Count your blessings

This book belongs to

_____

Written by Stephen Barnett
Illustrated by Rosie Brooks

Contents

About this book

The stories in this book enlightens children with the qualities of optimism, patience and treating others well. Questions at the end test the child's attention, and the new words encourage vocabulary building.

Count your blessings

We were sitting in a bus with mother when we overheard a man talking loudly. 'The weather is terrible,' he said. 'I hate the rain!'

'The other day, rain splashed on to my new shoes which were costly. And now I think I will throw them away,' he said, angrily.

Mother didn't say anything but gave us
the look that she uses when she is not
happy about something.

Later, when we had got off the bus and were walking to our house, our mother talked to us about the man on the bus.

'That man should be grateful for what he has,' she said. 'He should learn to count his blessings.'

'I agree that it is too wet sometimes. But without the rain we would not be able to grow our food or have the colourful flowers!'

'And spending so much money on a pair
of shoes and then grumbling about them
getting wet . . .'

10

'…is terrible when there are many people who can't afford to buy any shoes at all!' We walked on in silence thinking about this.

'I try to be content with what I have,' said mother, putting an arm around us. 'I count my blessings too. My blessings include the two of you!'

Have patience

'Have we reached?' We stretched on our seats in the train. 'I can't wait for the train trip to end,' I said.

'Don't be too impatient,' said father. 'I know you want to get to the farm. But if you become impatient, you will miss many wonderful things.'

We were puzzled. 'What do you mean?' I asked.

'Well, the train can't go any faster and we won't get to the farm any quicker by being annoyed. So try to enjoy what's happening right now.'

'Look out of the window,' said father. 'Try to enjoy the journey.'

We settled back in our seats and watched what was passing by outside. We dozed in the sunshine, ate the sandwiches that mother had made for our trip.

'Children, we've reached!' said father.
'Already?!' said my sister.

Treat others as you would like to be treated

We were in a shop with our uncle, waiting to pay for our groceries. In the front row, a customer was behaving rudely with the woman packing the groceries.

'Come on, come on!' shouted the man.
'Hurry up! I haven't got all day!'

'Excuse me,' my uncle called out to the man. 'You shouldn't be so rude to people. How would you like if someone shouted at you like that?'

'That was a rude man,' our uncle said.
Sometimes all of us get a little annoyed at
things. But we must be careful about how
we treat people.

The next day, as I was about to go
biking, the old lady next door called out.
'Simon, can you please help me to lift
something?'

Oh no, this was annoying! I thought I'll
pretend that I hadn't heard her and keep
on going. But then I remembered what
my uncle had said.

I put my bike against the wall and went
up the path to her door. 'How can I help
you?' I asked.

The work didn't take long and then I was
on my way. I was glad to have helped
the old lady.

One day when I will be old, maybe I will also ask for help from someone younger. And I'll be glad if they help me then.

New words

terrible

puzzled

watched

grumbling

annoyed

angrily

biking

blessings

colourful

content

customer

enjoy

excuse

farm

front

grateful

groceries

impatient

journey

pay

pretend

rain

remembered

rude

sandwiches

silence

snail

splashed

sunshine

thinking

train

treat

trip

weather

wet

window

wonderful

overheard

weather

include

afford

stretched

What did you learn?

Count your blessings
What had happened to the man's shoes?
What does it mean to count your blessings?

Have patience
Where were the children going by train?
What did the father say to the children to do to enjoy
the trip?

Treat others as you would like to be treated
Whom did the child go to the shop with?
What did the child do to help the old lady?